90 day approval
10-15-90
14.95

A Grass Green Gallop

Books by Patricia Hubbell

THE TIGERS BROUGHT PINK LEMONADE

A GRASS GREEN GALLOP

Come: Let us watch horses together—
Colts playing, mares grazing.
Let us step quietly over the grass.
Let every shade of green cover the hillsides
And the wind rush in our ears.

Poems by Patricia Hubbell
Illustrations by Ronald Himler

ATHENEUM 1990 NEW YORK

For Howard C. Raven, D. V. M.

P. H.

For Billy, Katie, and Jeannie
in grass green New Jersey

R. H.

Atheneum
Macmillan Publishing Company
866 Third Avenue, New York, NY 10022
Collier Macmillan Canada, Inc.
First Edition
Printed in Hong Kong

Library of Congress Cataloging-in-Publication Data
Hubbell, Patricia.
A grass green gallop : poems / by Patricia Hubbell; illustrations by Ronald Himler.—1st ed. p. cm.
Summary: A collection of poems celebrating the beauty, motion, and sounds of horses, from newborn foals, to Thoroughbreds, to old cart horses.
ISBN 0-689-31604-6
1. Horses—Juvenile poetry. 2. Children's poetry, American. [1. Horses—Poetry. 2. American poetry.] I. Himler, Ronald, ill. II. Title.
PS3558.U22G73 1990 811'.54—dc20
89-36354 CIP AC

Contents

The Foal

A saddlebred foal…

p l
m i
u n
a j g p l
a i
e n
a l g

a puppet-on-a-string-ling
a bird-on-the-wing-ling
a bushy-tailed stripling
goes grasshopper leaping
goes hopping
not walking

then suddenly he's walking,
he's standing,
he's ducking
his head between flanks
and he's standing and nursing
he's sucking and tugging
he's pulling and tugging
then he

a p
e s
l from his dam
and his nose is all milky…
he's off like a Cricket,
a long-legged leapling.

Before the Jumping Class, at Old Salem, Saturday Night

The equitation riders flock about the fences,
like sandpipers pacing off the shore.
With quick, exaggerated steps they turn
from fence to fence around the ring,
black legs as stiff as birds',
black velvet caps that catch the light
as feathers catch the morning sun.
They step and pause, recheck and back,
stride on. They wheel, as one,
and exit out the gate,
returning, not on their own wings,
but on the Pegasus of each one's dreams.

Appaloosa Pony

Your spots
are like berries,
sunk in the dough
of your fatness.
Like sunlight through oak leaves,
you dazzle me,
my muffin-child,
my stripe-hooved galloper.
You stand in oak shade
and I cannot find you.
Popcorn covers your rump.
Like a hunter in camouflage,
you slip through the trees.
Your spots turn to shadows,
shifting through pegboard.
Submerged in the depths
of dapple and shadow,
your whinny,
a quivering arrow of sound,
sonars me to you.

At the Driving Show

Horses and ponies, under the trees,
Jack Russell terriers sniffing the breeze.
A team of fat Belgians hitched to a wagon,
A high-stepping Morgan that snorts like a dragon.
Two bays hitched up tandem and taut in the traces,
Someone's dun pony that's off to the races.
A pair of brown hackneys, alike as two peas,
A steel-gray cob (slightly in at the knees).
A strawberry roan, named "The Duchess of Kent,"
—you and I visiting, under the tent.

The Fight

Jake says: "It's time to teach that colt to drive."
The colt has other plans. *He* says he'll strive

to land old Jake in berry patch or pond.
To tell the truth, he's never been too fond

of even being ridden. It's a drag
you have to put up with. He'd lug or lag

but all it gets you is a whipping. Yet,
he'd love to see old Jake climb, dripping wet,

out of that pond. He'd chance the whip for that!

On Tuesday, Jake, cocksure, hitches up the colt.
No long rein work for him. "He'll never bolt,"

says Jake (whose confidence is seldom low).
"This won't be any kind of fight. He'll go

right where I tell him to. You'll see he will.
I'll take him up beside the pond. Hold still...

Now, off we go...Now, take it easy...WHOA!"

A half mile off they feel the jolt.
Round One: The Colt.

One Little Colt

One little colt, alone on the hill,
heard the wind shout, "Run!"
So he ran down the hill.

One little colt, alone by the stream,
heard the water gurgle, "Go!"
So he dashed across the stream.

One little colt, alone by the wall,
heard the cow moo, "Leap!"
so he leaped across the wall.

One little colt, alone by the gate,
heard the goat blat, "Sidle!"
so he sidled through the gate.

One little colt, prancing through the heather,
heard one little boy shout,
"Now we're together!"

The Family Horse

Do you like this gray?
He's a family horse.
    A long-backed,
    high-hipped,
    family horse.
Is he kind?
  Of course. He's a family horse.

When you canter, you feel his rocking-horse gait,
and you know if you push him, you'll never be late,
for he'll canter from Westport right on to New York.
                                        He's a family horse.

You don't need a saddle when you ride him.
Just take a leap and you're astride him.
    There's room for Sue
    and Mary-Lou
    and Uncle Jim
    and Me
    and You.
He's a long-backed, strong-backed, high-hipped, he-never-nipped
                                        family horse.
—And—
He'll-never-run-away-no-he'll-never-run-away-oh-he'll-never-
ever-ever-ever-ever-run-away-he's-a-
                                        family...WHOA!...horse.

Mare and Colt

She's teaching him the tricks—
how to outwit the taming hand,
how, if you stretch your neck,
you can reach the McIntosh
in the old tree by the well,
or (for windfalls) splay
your forelegs wide,
snake your head
under the lowest rail.
She's teaching him how,
when the hand with the halter reaches,
to parry and duck and elude,
and—Rule Number One—
how (when you *want* to)
to nicker up,
big-eyed and calm,
lipping the sugar
from the outstretched palm.

The Standardbred

Along the fence, the Standardbred,
Retired from racing ages back,
Paces, restless, through the days.
His steady rounds have traced a track
That bears into the grass and daisies.
Day after day, he makes the loop;
Adjusts his speed to suit each lap,
From gate to apple tree, and off.
Stride lengthening, he hits the stretch
And races down the orchard rows.
He paces swiftly past the trees—
And beats his shadow by a nose.

October

I ride the plumed October,
The swift and lofty steed,
His mane is gold-encrusted
And jeweled are his eyes;
He sweeps a tail of rubies,
His bridle flashes fair,
    But Oh below I hear his hooves
        Hollow on the air.
His nostrils spew white hoarfrost,
His eyes spurt bits of flame,
He rears and strikes the treetops
And snorts the leaves away;
I cling the high October
And vault him through the days,
    But Oh below his hollow hooves
        Strike ice upon the lanes.

The Pony on Halloween

A Shetland pony,
dark brown
and in full winter coat,
escaped from his paddock
one Halloween
and wandered
into town.
Sending running:
  Three witches,
  one goblin,
  two clowns,
  and a truck driver
  from Canada,
  who hurriedly
  climbed into his cab,
  shouting:
        "Bear! Bear! Bear!"
Upon which,
the Shetland
trotted back
to his pen
and smugly whinnied:
        "I may be Woolly and Small—
        But I tricked them All!"

Horses in the Rain

North of Narragansett, where the sea gnaws at the fields,
I saw three gray horses, grazing in the rain.
As sea runs through sand, fingers of water,
touching new places, stroked their flanks.
On the bay, three sailboats wheeled and ran for home.
A flock of gulls beat down the wind.
Anchored to their field, the horses rode out the squall—
Rain slicked the black manes ropy,
turned the tails to wind-frayed hawsers.
Shut in my car, I watched one dappled mare fling her head high.
I named them:
"Sea Grass," "Beach Plum," "The Wild-Eyed Rose."

"Doc"

Doc's Trakehner,
17.1 hands high,
rises to the wall—
Muscled like a flooding river,
she flows, touches earth, springs on.
Doc watches.
In his mind,
a leg's thrown over her:
No gloves, of course—
He never could abide
to ride in gloves—
They got between
you and the horse,
as now his raspy breath
gets in the way of...

Nothing.

Forget it.

A new horse—
That's the ticket—
For all the years
that you were vet
to a whole county and beyond,
you saw, in your mind's eye,
a mare like this.

Move on. Move on.

The Trakehner
has cleared the course.
Doc wheels his dusty Chevrolet
across the field.
His blue eyes warm:

"She can do it!"

Poem for a Friend

If you had never driven a team,
   loved rose-gray stipple, dapple, bay,
      the hunt team galloping the hill,
         the polo pony, Percheron, or foal in field—
If you and I had never once talked horse,
   or laughed and joked, as, leaning on the rail,
      we watched these ponies school,
         you still would be my friend—
         This common ground is only where we met.

Ten Valentines for a Horse

A carrot, and an apple tart,
a lightly-laden, well-greased cart,

A pasture in a gentle rain,
an extra scoop of luscious grain.

A canter through the soft beach sand,
a firm and gentle, caring hand

that strokes your neck and rubs your nose.
Deep, golden straw in which to doze

and watch the fading sunset light.
A well-known voice across the night

that makes you stamp, and prick your ears.
—Safe passage through the years.

Carriage Team

Jangling chain and squeak of leather,
Heads held high, we wheel together.

(Carriage window veiled in lace,
Carnations in the crystal vase,

Harness tooled and trimmed in brass—)
Foam flecks our chests, and as we pass

The people cheer. "—Heads up! Stand clear!"
We hardly deign to flick an ear.

Fetlocks trimmed of every feather,
Tails plumed, we wheel together.

At the Horse Show

Jennifer Rose,
  on her big dun horse,
  gallops the local hunter course.
Jennifer's horse, "The Paddock's Pride,"
  takes the in-and-out in his stride.
  He clears the hedge. He clears the stile.
  He gallops gaily the full half mile.
He's a lop-eared dun with a Roman nose,
But—"Looks aren't *all,*" says Jennifer Rose.
The judges mark their books and smile.
They pin the blue to his gleaming bridle.
Jennifer rubs his homely nose—
  "He's a lovely horse," says Jennifer Rose.

Charley

No gentleman, this horse was most unkind,
With wicked eye, and wickeder behind,
Recalcitrant, and oft inclined to buck—
"Unsalable!" his owner cursed. "Worst luck!"

The World Turned Horses

Do you remember when you first loved horses?
How their hugeness filled your grandfather's barn?
How, at night in the old house,
your dreams grew loud with neighing?
Do you remember, that year when you were six,
How your grandfather lifted you
high through shadowed air,
to the back of the great Percheron
stomping in the last, dim stall?
Do you remember that first gripping of the knees,
and how all the world turned horses,
horses everywhere,
flying through the golden dust?
Do you remember that day,
that day when your hands grew reins?

Plain Jane

I knew a black mare
And her name was Jane,
Plain Jane, Plain Jane.

Carry me over the houses, Jane,
Carry me over the cities and forests,
Gallop the skies with me, Jane.
Over the sunrise,
Over the sunset,
Over the nebulae
into infinity.
Carry me out of constraint, Jane,
Gallop me into the next dimension.

Feeding Time

Whicker,
Whinny,
Nicker,
Neigh—

At four,
all horses
call for hay—

Molly, Tortoise,
Buck, and Finney,
Up and down the aisles
they whinny.

The grooms
toss in
the shining flakes—

Like children
eating birthday cakes,
the horses feast—

There's not a sound,
Oh, not a flicker—

Of Whinny,
Whicker,
Neigh,
Or Nicker.

The Cart Horse in August

Down 57th Street, the cart horse comes.
He left the bums at 81st. Now,
he joins the world of elegance and grace.
Hitched, like a hackney, to a hansom cab,
he's still a drab, old, tired wreck of horse—
but valiant as a hunter in the field.
He tries to sidle, but can only plod.
His driver sticks a flower in his bridle
and clicks him on, to face Fifth Avenue.
The cart horse lifts his head, to look his best,
and please.
A wheel hits the curb. He stumbles to his knees.
—Please, God, have pastures where the poor may rest.

The Percheron

Like a great boulder,
the Percheron sleeps...
When, at last, he stands,
it is as if the earth rose up
and stone grew legs.
Across the trembling field he steps.
Where he lay, only the shadow
of his sleep remains,
quivering the bent, blue grass.

To Freckles, at 29

Horse, who has carried me many times
Farther than wonder, I ask you to
Trust me, and come to my whistle.
  Hear me, and come.
The sun is a fortress
That guards us from darkness.
  Trust me, and come.
Your name is a whisper
The trees know the sound of—
  Hear me, and come.

Plea of the Old Horse on Looking through the Kitchen Window

I have shed my winter coat
and you have not blanketed me—

a warm spell in early March—
I shed too early.

It is cold in the barn now.
Dampness climbs into my ears.

I am shivering, Miss.
Come, and blanket me.

If you will not blanket me,
Will you bring me a carrot?

I see you through the window,
warm at your stove.

I see the carrots.
Won't you come, please, Miss,

Come to blanket me?
Come with a carrot?

Prairie Plow Horse

If bravery
is moving on
in spite of fear,
  this horse is brave.
Born earlier than spring,
  he staggered to his feet
  in snow and wind,
  and lost his dam
  (before the ending
  of that first cold hour)
  to fever and to chill.
Found by chance
and carried to the barn,
he feared the smell of man,
but lived with man.
Fearing the wind,
he worked in wind.
Hating snow,
snow was his home.
When blizzards came,
  he shrilled his whinny to the sky
  and turned to pull the plow
  until the roads were clear.
Now, in the cold and rain of this December day,
he walks, on a loose lead,
up to the pit.

Pony in Moonlight

I trot through wet grass
when the moon is high,
shadow and rock,
moon and I,
and an owl hoots by.

I feel cool moonlight
touch my back.
The owl's wing brushes
the tamarack.
I feel the hush
of a quivering thrush
hidden in timothy,
waving, lush,
and the owl hoots by.

I stamp the turf
as moonlight drips
in double dapples
across my hips.
I wake the air
with my shrillest neigh—
and the owl hoots by.

The Thoroughbred

A Thoroughbred,
too small for the track,
hooty as an owl,
skittery as swallows,
she stepped with jittery hooves.
Three steps and she was foam—
foam on her flanks,
her outsized chest,
foam running down her shanks,
frothing on the coronet.
One August day,
on the ridge above the stream,
scooting faster than a hooked trout,
she staggered and nearly fell,
caught herself, shook,
whinnied once—raced on:
A Thoroughbred,
too small for the track.

The Ride

Silent in the morning,
Silent through the day,
Silent on the white horse
galloping away—
Silent in the evening,
Silent through the night,
Silent on the black horse
that takes me to the light—
Silent on the long ride,
Speaking only to the wind—
Earth, that holds these hoofbeats—
Did you know I passed?

The Workhorse

Nearly dusk, in the hills of Vermont,
the wide road, snaking toward Bennington:
  He came up like a ghost,
  a boy on a gray Percheron,
  riding her home in the dusk.
  His bare feet hung white from his jeans.
  Dreamily, he toed her sides.
  In a glance, we could see it all—
  The feathered fetlocks, like white birds fluffing,
  the coarse mane, all askew,
  his slim, still hand on her neck,
  the quietness.

A Grass Green Gallop

Gallop
the
grass
  my green horse   my young one
    in your costume of wind,
                                        gallop the grass,
    in your song of whinnies,
                                        gallop the grass,
    in your strength of bucking,
                                        gallop the grass,
gallop the know-nothing grass of April
my rearer
my leaper
my bridle-resister

gallop the green grass
O the grass green gallop